COOKING
THE
AUSTRIAN
WAY

To my cooking teacher, Frau Anna Merighi, whose favorite saying was "Liebe geht durch den Magen," ("Love goes through the stomach")

Lerner Publications Company,
A division of Lerner Publishing Group
241 First Avenue North
Minneapolis, MN 55401 U.S.A.

Website address: www.lernerbooks.com

Library of Congress Cataloging-in-Publication Data

Hughes, Helga.
    Cooking the Austrian way / by Helga Hughes.—Rev. and expanded.
      p. cm. — (Easy menu ethnic cookbooks)
    Summary: An introduction to the cooking of Austria including such traditional recipes as Wiener schnitzel, potato noodles, and Sacher cake. Also includes information on the geography, customs, and people of this European country.
    ISBN: 0–8225–4102–5 (lib. bdg. : alk. paper)
    1. Cookery, Austrian—Juvenile literature. 2. Austria—Social life and customs—Juvenile literature. [1. Cookery, Austrian. 2. Austria—Social life and customs.] I. Title. II. Series.
TX721 .H82 2004
641.59436—dc21
                                         2002152146

Manufactured in the United States of America
1 2 3 4 5 6 – JR – 09 08 07 06 05 04

COOKING

THE

AUSTRIAN

WAY

revised and expanded

to include new low-fat

and vegetarian recipes

Helga Hughes

Lerner Publications Company • Minneapolis

Contents

Introduction

Austrian cuisine typifies the saying that "variety is the spice of life." Throughout Austrian history, different groups of people settled in the country, and each group brought its own customs and cuisine. As the various groups mixed, they helped shape Austrian culture. In ancient times, Celts and Romans settled in Austria, and the country became part of the Roman Empire. Later, various Germanic groups and Magyars (Hungarians) settled there. Austria had various rulers until the tenth century A.D., when the Babenberg family gained control. The Babenbergs ruled for two hundred years, and Vienna became an important trading center during their reign.

Crusaders (Christian soldiers who fought to win Palestine from the Muslims during the eleventh, twelfth, and thirteenth centuries) stopped in Vienna on their way home from the Middle East. They brought sugarcane, muscat, and spices such as pepper, ginger, cinnamon, cloves, and nutmeg, which Austrians incorporated into their foods.

In 1278 the powerful Habsburg family took control of Austria and acquired surrounding regions. In 1683, under Habsburg rule, Austria

Austrian cooking is influenced by many world cuisines. A hearty Austrian dinner might include paprika chicken (recipe on page 37), potato noodles (recipe on page 42), and egg custard soup (recipe on page 36).

conquered Hungary and became the center of a huge and powerful empire. Austrian cooking was influenced yet again—by foods from Romania and the former republics of Czechoslovakia and Yugoslavia.

During the 1700s and 1800s, famous composers such as Mozart and Haydn lived in Austria. The Habsburgs ruled this cultural center, the Austrian Empire, for six hundred years, until its downfall during World War I (1914–1918). The empire consisted of more than fifty million people and included twelve nationalities. Many of Austria's famous recipes developed as a result of this long and complex history.

The Land and Its People

Austria is only about the size of Maine, but it has a population of more than 7.5 million people—approximately six times the population of Maine. Austria is bordered by Switzerland and

Liechtenstein to the west; Germany, the Czech Republic, and Slovakia to the north; Hungary to the east; and Slovenia and Italy to the south.

The Alps stretch across the western, southern, and central parts of Austria and form the dominant feature of the country. In many places, beautiful, green valleys lie between the mountains. Austria also has many lovely lakes and dense forests. Austria's scenic beauty attracts millions of tourists each year.

Vienna, the capital of Austria and its largest city, lies on the Danube River. Other large Austrian cities include Salzburg, Innsbruck, Linz, and Graz.

Like the United States, the heritage of Austria has been enriched by the mixture of many different cultures. In Austria most city dwellers live in apartment buildings. Town and village residents usually live in single-family homes. However, housing styles vary from region to region. German, the official language of Austria, is spoken by 98 percent of the people.

Austrians' lifestyles reflect their rich history. They are proud that Austria continues to be a leading cultural center of Europe. Most Austrians enjoy art, music, outdoor sports, and good food. Austrians also place great importance on the preparation of their food.

Regional Cooking

Wiener schnitzel is probably Austria's most popular dish. In the movie *The Sound of Music*, set in Austria, Julie Andrews even sings that schnitzel and noodles are one of her favorite things. Yet each of Austria's nine provinces (Burgenland, Carinthia, Lower Austria, Salzburg, Styria, Tirol, Upper Austria, the city of Vienna, and Vorarlberg) claims fame for a culinary specialty.

Both Lower Austria, the chief wine-producing area of the country, and Vienna are renowned for their coffeehouses and delicious pastries.

People in Styria, a southeastern province, prepare hearty meals, such as *Fridatten*, a soup made from sliced, rolled pancakes in a bouillon broth, or *Styrisches Schweineres*, a one-pot stew.

The southernmost province is Carinthia, where Austria's highest peak, the 12,641-foot (3,853-meter) Gross Glockner is located. Many inns still use old family recipes to cook fish and game, which are abundant in this province. Nothing is wasted—not even the bones, which are used for broth. Carinthians are also proud of the many kinds of noodles they offer—savory noodles filled with ham, bacon, mushrooms, or cottage cheese, as well as sweet noodles filled with dried fruit and covered with melted butter and sugar.

Salzburg, the smallest province and birthplace of Mozart, is best known for music. However, it is also acclaimed for its *Nockerln*, a sweet dessert soufflé.

The southwestern province of Tirol is famous for its cheese, perhaps because the grazing pastures for the cows are so high in the mountains. The *Bergbauern* (mountain peasants) also make *Bauernspeck* (smoked peasants' bacon) in winter. This bacon plays a major role in Austrian cooking since it is used in salads, soups, sauerkraut, dumplings, and other foods.

Besides the cuisine of the various provinces, Austrian cooking has also been influenced by Czech, Slovakian, German, and Hungarian foods. They add to the variety and flavor of many Austrian dishes.

Holidays and Festivals

Holidays and festivals play a very important role in Austrian life. About 80 percent of Austrians are Roman Catholic, so many holidays and festivals reflect this. Other Austrians are Protestant, Jewish, Greek and Russian Orthodox, or Muslim. Every province in Austria honors a particular saint and celebrates its own saint's day. Austrians also hold other festivals to celebrate such events as seasons or harvests. In summer big cities such as Salzburg and Vienna hold major arts festivals.

Holiday parade participants and some audience members dress in traditional lederhosen and dirndls.

On holidays some Austrians dress in traditional national or regional outfits. Men and boys wear lederhosen, short trousers gathered just below the knee. Women and girls wear dirndls—outfits consisting of a bright blouse, skirt, and apron.

Probably the most important, unforgettable, and magical holiday of the year in Austria is Christmas. Cities sparkle with holiday lights and ornamented trees, and outdoor music concerts abound. Colorful markets, smelling of roasted chestnuts, *Gluhwein* (hot spiced wine), and *Punsch* (wine-spiked fruit punch), are set up all over city centers. At the markets, vendors sell a huge variety of crafts, drinks, and foods including pretzels, candies and other sweets, and fluffy pancakes shredded and served with stewed plums. Potato fritters, strudels, sausages, and the traditional *Lebkuchen*—usually made with gingerbread, cinnamon, honey, and orange or lemon peels—are also served.

Colorful desserts, including pastries, fruit breads, cakes, and other sweets, are beautifully displayed in pastry shops and are prepared in homes during the festive Christmas season. These delicacies include cookies such as Lebkuchen; *Vanillekipferl*, or vanilla crescents; and *Zimtsterne*, or cinnamon stars, made with almonds, lemon juice, and cinnamon.

Christmas festivities begin early in Austria. Four weeks before Christmas, Austrians hang wreaths made from evergreen twigs twined with red ribbon from their ceilings. Four red candles are set in a circle, and on the fourth Sunday before Christmas, one candle is lit, on the third Sunday, two candles are lit, and by the Sunday before Christmas, all four are burning.

For Nikolaustag (St. Nicholas Day, December 6), a person dressed as St. Nicholas, wearing a long robe, walks through city markets and village centers, passing out sweets to children. Krampus, a monsterlike figure, usually accompanies St. Nicholas. Parents teasingly tell their children that if they don't behave, Krampus will take them away with him.

Austrians celebrate Christmas Eve, December 24, by unveiling an elegantly decorated Christmas tree and exchanging presents. Families sing carols, particularly Austria's favorite and most famous carol, "Silent Night," written in Austria in the early 1800s. Austrian families sit down to a large, festive meal, traditionally of fried carp (a type of fish) served with potato balls, cucumber salad, and mushroom rice. In some regions, roast pork or Wiener schnitzel is the traditional Christmas Eve dinner. After dinner some Austrian families attend Midnight Mass at church.

Christmas Day is a holy day for resting, quiet celebration, or attending church services. Austrians usually enjoy a long dinner with family and friends. A traditional Christmas Day dinner includes roast goose, red cabbage, potato dumplings, and a variety of Christmas breads and sweets. Austrians often continue the celebration to December 26 with elaborate meals and visits from family and friends. Many people, especially those who live in cities, also attend musical concerts and other performances.

On New Year's Eve, people merrily shoot off fireworks throughout the country at midnight. In Vienna a huge party takes place in front of famous St. Stephen's Cathedral. Some partygoers gather there and wait for the church bell to ring at midnight. Then they pop open their champagne bottles and light fireworks. Vienna's streets come alive during this holiday with music under tents and vendors selling snacks. Orchestra, opera, and symphony concerts take place, including the traditional New Year's Day Vienna Philharmonic Concert. An elegant New Year's dinner might include lemon soup, duck, potato baskets, apple salad, pastries, and coffee. It is customary to give friends and relatives good-luck charms for the New Year. Charms include marzipan pigs—a dessert made of almond paste, sugar, and egg whites and shaped into adorable pig faces—and small sponge cake cookies in the shape of fish. The recipient must bite the head off the fish first for good luck.

Austria's Christians celebrate Heilige Drei Könige, or Epiphany, on January 6. The holiday commemorates how three Wise Men from the East looked for the newly born Jesus. Children dress as the Three Wise

Men, usually in long white nightshirts and crowns painted gold. They go from house to house singing and asking for gifts of food. Their neighbors reward them with cookies or chocolate.

In late winter, most Austrians celebrate Carnival (called Fasching in German) to symbolically chase away the evil spirits of winter. People play music, dress in costumes, parade with decorated floats, dance, and hold parties. In Vienna the most famous and glorious events of Fasching are the balls. These elegant, formal dances are held throughout the season in huge dance halls. Almost every profession—including hunters, police officers, and bakers—holds a ball. There is even a children's ball. *Faschingskrapfen*, a kind of doughnut with jam, is a common sight in storefronts during this time.

The merriment of Fasching comes to an end on Aschermittwoch (Ash Wednesday), the beginning of the forty days of Lent, or the solemn time of fasting before Easter. Meat, eggs, and dairy products are forbidden during Lent, but strict fasting is rare in Austria. On Aschermittwoch, many Austrians still eat *Heringschmaus*, pickled herring and onions, since fish is allowed during Lent.

Easter falls in March or April. It commemorates both springtime and the Christian belief in Jesus Christ rising from the dead. As with other holidays in Austria, food plays a prominent role. Main courses for Easter dinner include whole pig, ham, lamb, or rabbit. Pastries and breads are also a big part of Easter meals, including bread with raisins baked in twisted or braided strands. After the meal, coffee and Sacher torte, a delicious cake made with chocolate and apricot jam, may be served.

In May and June, Vienna holds a large musical arts festival. For more than a month in late summer, Salzburg holds its art festival, with thousands of performances including theater, opera, music concerts, and street performances.

In September Austrians who live in rural areas celebrate good harvests. During harvest festivals, people decorate the altars of village churches with fruits, grains, and flowers. Processions are led by animals who are decorated with wreaths and flowers, pulling carts of large wreaths of grains.

Thriving vineyards, such as this one in Styria, provide grapes for Austrian wines. The wine harvest is celebrated each fall.

Among the merriest celebrations in Austria are vintage festivals, celebrated in wine-producing areas, usually in early October. These festivals celebrate the year's grape harvest and wine making. Villagers hang bunches of grapes around town, play music, and sing and dance in the streets. They decorate the markets with huge wine casks.

Austrians celebrate Allerheiligen (All Saints' Day) on November 1. This Christian holy day commemorates all the saints of the Church. The next day, November 2, is Allerseelen (All Souls' Day), a time to honor the dead. Austrians carry burning candles and dried flowers to the graves of loved ones. In parts of the province of Tirol, in southwestern Austria, it is a custom to leave food out overnight on the kitchen table for the dead who may return on that day.

Martinstag (St. Martin's Day) is celebrated on November 11, mostly in the province of Burgenland, in eastern Austria. This holiday honors St. Martin, a monk who lived in the fourth century. The goose is the animal symbol of St. Martin, and traditional meals of roast goose are served on this day. Ceremonies and parades take place, often with children displaying homemade paper or wooden lanterns.

Before You Begin

Cooking any dish, plain or fancy, is easier and more fun if you are familiar with its ingredients. Austrian cooking uses some ingredients that you may not know. You should be familiar with the special terms that will be used in various recipes in this book. Therefore, before you start cooking any of the Austrian dishes in this book, study the following "dictionary" of utensils, terms, and special ingredients very carefully. Then read through each recipe you want to try from beginning to end.

You are then ready to shop for ingredients and to organize the cookware you will need. Once you have assembled everything, you can begin to cook. It is also important to read "The Careful Cook" before you start. Following these rules will make your cooking experience safe, fun, and easy.

Trout Vienna Style (recipe on page 41) and broccoli salad with bacon (recipe on page 45) make an attractive and nutritious meal.

The Careful Cook

Whenever you cook, there are certain safety rules you must always keep in mind. Even experienced cooks follow these rules when they are in the kitchen.

- Always wash your hands before handling food. Thoroughly wash all raw vegetables and fruits to remove dirt, chemicals, and insecticides. Wash uncooked poultry, fish, and meat under cold water.
- Use a cutting board when cutting up vegetables and fruits. Don't cut them up in your hand! And be sure to cut in a direction *away* from you and your fingers.
- Long hair or loose clothing can easily catch fire if brought near the burners of a stove. If you have long hair, tie it back before you start cooking.
- Turn all pot handles toward the back of the stove so that you will not catch your sleeves or jewelry on them. This is especially important when younger brothers and sisters are around. They could easily knock off a pot and get burned.
- Always use a pot holder to steady hot pots or to take pans out of the oven. Don't use a wet cloth on a hot pan because the steam it produces could burn you.
- Lift the lid of a steaming pot with the opening away from you so that you will not get burned.
- If you get burned, hold the burn under cold running water. Do not put grease or butter on it. Cold water helps to take the heat out, but grease or butter will only keep it in.
- If grease or cooking oil catches fire, throw baking soda or salt at the bottom of the flame to put it out. (Water will *not* put out a grease fire.) Call for help, and try to turn all the stove burners to "off."

Cooking Utensils

bread pan—A baking pan in the shape of a loaf of bread

colander—A bowl with holes in the bottom and sides. It is used for draining liquid from solid food.

double boiler—Two saucepans that fit together so the contents in the upper pan can be heated by boiling water in the lower pan

grater—A utensil with sharp-edged holes, used to grate food into small pieces

potato ricer—A utensil in which foods are pressed through small holes to produce pieces in the shape of rice grains

rolling pin—A cylindrical tool used for rolling out dough

sieve—A bowl-shaped utensil made of wire or plastic mesh, used to wash or drain small, fine foods

slotted spoon—A spoon with small openings in the bowl. It is used to remove solid food from liquid.

springform pan—A pan with a detachable rim

steaming basket—A metal basket that fits inside a saucepan and allows food to be cooked with steam

whisk—A wire utenstil used for beating food by hand

Cooking Terms

beat—To stir rapidly in a circular motion

boil—To heat a liquid over high heat until bubbles form and rise rapidly to the surface

brown—To cook food quickly over high heat so that the surface turns an even brown

dice—To chop food into small, square pieces

fold—To blend an ingredient with other ingredients by using a gentle, overturning circular motion instead of by stirring or beating

garnish—To decorate with small pieces of food, such as chopped parsley

grate—To cut into tiny pieces by rubbing the food against a grater

hard-boil—To cook an egg in its shell until both the yolk and the white are firm

marinate—To soak a food in a seasoned liquid

pinch—A very small amount, usually what you can pick up between your thumb and forefinger

preheat—To allow an oven to warm up to a certain temperature before putting food into it

sauté—To fry in a small amount of oil or other fat, stirring or turning the food to prevent burning

sift—To put an ingredient, such as flour or sugar, through a sifter to break up any lumps

simmer—To cook over low heat in liquid kept just below its boiling point. Bubbles may occasionally rise to the surface.

steam—To cook food with the steam from boiling water

whip—To beat an ingredient, such as cream or egg whites, until light and fluffy

Special Ingredients

apple cider vinegar—A vinegar made from apple cider

bay leaf—The dried leaf of the bay tree (also called European laurel)

bittersweet chocolate—Dark chocolate made with less sugar than milk chocolate

bouillon cube—A compressed mixture of spices, seasoning, oils, and often a meat extract, used to make broth and add flavor to other foods

bread crumbs—Pieces of stale bread broken into small chunks by crushing the bread with a rolling pin or the bottom of a glass. Grocery stores sell packaged bread crumbs.

buttermilk—Cultured milk made by adding a certain bacteria to sweet milk

chives—A member of the onion family. The thin, green stalks are chopped and used as a garnish and a flavoring.

cinnamon—A spice made from the bark of a tree in the laurel family. It is available ground and in sticks.

farina—A fine meal made from grain. It is used chiefly for puddings or as a breakfast cereal.

garlic—An herb whose distinctive flavor is used in many dishes. Each bulb can be broken up into several small sections called cloves. Most recipes use only one or two cloves. Before chopping a garlic clove, remove its papery covering.

nutmeg—A fragrant spice that is often used in ground form in desserts

paprika—A red seasoning made from the dried, ground pods of the capsicum pepper plant. It adds hot or sweet flavor to foods.

parsley—A green, leafy herb used as a seasoning and as a garnish

slivered almonds—Almonds that have been split into thin strips

spicy brown mustard—A condiment made from mustard seeds, vinegar, seasoning, and spices

tarragon vinegar—A vinegar made from a blend of distilled wine vinegars, salt, sugar, herbs, spices, and fragrant tarragon leaves. Tarragon is a European wormwood plant.

vanilla extract—A liquid made from vanilla beans that is used to flavor food

Healthy and Low-fat Cooking Tips

Many modern cooks are concerned about preparing healthy, low-fat meals. Here are a few simple ways to reduce the fat content of the recipes in this book. Specific suggestions for individual recipes appear throughout the book. Don't worry, they'll still taste delicious!

Many recipes call for butter or oil to fry meats, vegetables, or other ingredients. Using oil lowers fat right away, but you can also reduce the amount of oil you use. You can substitute a low-fat or nonfat cooking spray. Sprinkling a little salt on the vegetables brings out their natural juices, so you need less oil. Use a nonstick frying pan if you decide to use less butter or oil than the recipe calls for.

Substitute margarine for butter. Before making this substitution, consider the recipe. If it is a dessert, it's often best to use butter. Margarine may change the taste or consistency of the food.

Dairy products can be a source of unwanted fat. Replace heavy cream with half-and-half. Use fat-free evaporated milk instead of sweetened condensed milk. Many cheeses are available in reduced-fat or nonfat varieties, but these often don't melt as well. Reduce fat by using low-fat or nonfat yogurt in place of sour cream. Another easy way to reduce the fat from cheese is simply to use less of it. To avoid losing flavor, try using a stronger-tasting cheese.

Meat is an essential part of many Austrian meals. Some cooks replace ground beef with ground turkey, tofu, or chicken to lower fat. This changes the flavor, so you may need to experiment a bit. Using extra-lean ground beef is also an easy way to reduce fat.

When recipes call for chicken broth, use low-fat varieties or vegetable broth. Lower the cholesterol in dishes containing eggs by using an egg substitute.

Meals can be good for you and still taste great. As you become more experienced, try experimenting with recipes and substitutions to find the methods that work best for you.

METRIC CONVERSIONS

Cooks in the United States measure both liquid and solid ingredients using standard containers based on the 8-ounce cup and the tablespoon. These measurements are based on volume, while the metric system of measurement is based on both weight (for solids) and volume (for liquids). To convert from U.S. fluid tablespoons, ounces, quarts, and so forth to metric liters is a straightforward conversion, using the chart below. However, since solids have different weights—one cup of rice does not weigh the same as one cup of grated cheese, for example—many cooks who use the metric system have kitchen scales to weigh different ingredients. The chart below will give you a good starting point for basic conversions to the metric system.

MASS (weight)

1 ounce (oz.)	=	28.0 grams (g)
8 ounces	=	227.0 grams
1 pound (lb.) or 16 ounces	=	0.45 kilograms (kg)
2.2 pounds	=	1.0 kilogram

LIQUID VOLUME

1 teaspoon (tsp.)	=	5.0 milliliters (ml)
1 tablespoon (tbsp.)	=	15.0 milliliters
1 fluid ounce (oz.)	=	30.0 milliliters
1 cup (c.)	=	240 milliliters
1 pint (pt.)	=	480 milliliters
1 quart (qt.)	=	0.95 liters (l)
1 gallon (gal.)	=	3.80 liters

LENGTH

¼ inch (in.)	=	0.6 centimeters (cm)
½ inch	=	1.25 centimeters
1 inch	=	2.5 centimeters

TEMPERATURE

212°F	=	100°C (boiling point of water)
225°F	=	110°C
250°F	=	120°C
275°F	=	135°C
300°F	=	150°C
325°F	=	160°C
350°F	=	180°C
375°F	=	190°C
400°F	=	200°C

(To convert temperature in Fahrenheit to Celsius, subtract 32 and multiply by .56)

PAN SIZES

8-inch cake pan	=	20 x 4-centimeter cake pan
9-inch cake pan	=	23 x 3.5-centimeter cake pan
11 x 7-inch baking pan	=	28 x 18-centimeter baking pan
13 x 9-inch baking pan	=	32.5 x 23-centimeter baking pan
9 x 5-inch loaf pan	=	23 x 13-centimeter loaf pan
2-quart casserole	=	2-liter casserole

An Austrian Table

An Austrian cookbook published in 1846 stressed the importance of cleanliness in the kitchen and at the dining table, and this tradition is still observed. In many Austrian homes, tablecloths are changed daily, if not for each meal. Good cloths are hand-embroidered, and children often learn the art of embroidery. The edelweiss, a white flower that grows high in the Alps, and the *enzian*, another Alpine plant with yellow or blue flowers, are popular embroidery designs.

Hand-painted wooden egg holders are a feature of many Austrian breakfast tables. They are designed so that when the first boiled egg has been eaten, the holder is turned over to reveal a second egg.

Festive occasions often call for a centerpiece, possibly of fruits and nuts accented with peacock feathers—a reminder of when peacocks strutted through the splendid gardens of noble mansions. For less formal evening meals, wild cornflowers and poppies might decorate the table. The flowers are usually arranged in low vases to encourage cross-table conversation. Since evening meals often consist of open-faced sandwiches, wooden platters are often substituted for individual dinner plates at each setting. Hard rolls—very popular in Austria—are served in colored baskets, and butter and homemade spreads are served in ceramic bowls.

Austrians and tourists alike enjoy the mountain view from outdoor cafés in Salzburg.

An Austrian Menu

Below are two simplified menu plans for an Austrian dinner. One has meat as a main course, and one is vegetarian. Shopping lists of the necessary ingredients to prepare these meals are provided.

DINNER #1

Breaded veal

Cooked potato salad

Mixed green salad

Holiday fruit bread

SHOPPING LIST:

Produce

1 bunch parsley
2 lemons
3 large white potatoes
1 white onion
1 head of Bibb lettuce
1 bunch fresh spinach
1 green onion

Dairy/Egg/Meat

2 lb. leg of veal, cut into
  ¼-inch thick slices
3 eggs
3 slices of bacon
1 qt. buttermilk

Canned/Bottled/Boxed

2 chicken bouillon cubes
1 small jar sour pickles
apple cider vinegar
vegetable oil

Miscellaneous

salt
pepper
flour
bread crumbs
spicy brown mustard
white sugar
brown sugar
chopped nuts*
baking powder
1 c. prunes
baking soda
1 c. dates or figs
1 c. raisins

You can use walnuts, almonds, hazelnuts, or another kind of nut.

DINNER #2

Egg custard soup

Potato noodles

Cucumber salad

Salzburger sweet
soufflé

SHOPPING LIST:

Produce

1 bunch parsley
4 medium baking potatoes
2 large cucumbers
1 white onion
1 bunch chives
1 lemon

Dairy/Egg/Meat

1 qt. skim milk
1 dozen eggs
unsalted butter
16-oz. container sour cream
    or plain yogurt

Canned/Bottled/Boxed

4 vegetable bouillon cubes
vanilla extract
vegetable oil

Miscellaneous

salt
nutmeg
white pepper
flour
white sugar
3 tbsp. farina

Breakfast/Frühstück

For breakfast on workdays, most Austrians eat various types of rolls or coffee cakes, such as *Buchteln* (jelly rolls), *Schnecken* (snail-shaped rolls), *Striezel* (braided dough), or *Mozart Zopf* (dough that is braided in five strands, the way the famous composer wore his hair).

Many Austrians stop work to eat a second breakfast at about 10:00 A.M. This meal, called *Pause*, means "in between." It consists of at least two *Wienerlen*, the long, thin Vienna sausage, served with mustard on a hard roll. On weekends breakfast usually includes fresh fruit, cereals, hard rolls, soft-boiled eggs, dark bread with meats, such as *Leberwurst* (liver sausage), and cheeses.

In Austria the dough used to make coffee cakes is called *Germteig*. It is a homemade yeast dough, but you can buy something similar in most grocery stores. A one-pound package of frozen dinner roll dough can be substituted. Before starting the breakfast recipes in this chapter, thaw the amount of dough needed for three hours.

The spicy aroma of fresh-baked cinnamon and almond snails delights the senses (recipe on pages 32 and 33).

Jelly Rolls / Buchteln

Traditionally, these rolls are filled with plum jelly or jam, but raspberry, strawberry, or blackberry jam can also be used.

16 pieces of frozen dinner roll dough, thawed for 3 hours

1 c. plum jelly

4 tbsp. butter, melted*

powdered sugar

1. Place pieces of dough on a floured breadboard and cover with a towel (not terry cloth). Place in a warm spot (about 180°F) until dough has doubled in size (about 2½ hours).

2. Preheat oven to 350°F.

3. Grease a 10-inch springform pan and set aside.

4. On a lightly floured surface, roll each piece of dough into a 4-inch square.

5. Place 1 tbsp. of jelly or jam in the center of each square, moisten the edges with water, and pull up the corners, pinching together with fingers. Then pull up the sides and pinch seams shut.

6. Place rolls in springform pan, starting at the center and working around in circles. Brush generously with melted butter.

7. Cover with a towel (not terry cloth) and let rise for 15 to 20 minutes.

8. Remove towel and bake for 30 minutes, or until rolls are lightly browned.

9. Remove from oven, unclasp springform, and allow rolls to cool for 5 minutes.

10. Place rolls on a wire rack and sprinkle with powdered sugar.

11. When semi-cool, pull rolls apart and serve.

Waiting time (for dough to thaw): 3 hours
Additional waiting time (for dough to rise): 2¾ hours
Preparation time: 1½ hours
Baking time: 30 minutes
Makes 16 rolls

*To reduce the fat content of this dish, you can brush the rolls lightly with milk or with lightly beaten egg whites instead of with butter.

Cinnamon and Almond Snails/
Zimt und Mandelschnecken

6 pieces of frozen dinner roll dough, thawed for 3 hours

¼ c. almonds

7 tbsp. butter, melted

½ c. brown sugar

1 tbsp. cinnamon

1. Place pieces of dough on a floured breadboard, cover with a towel (not terry cloth), and place in a warm spot (about 180°F) until dough has doubled in size (about 2½ hours).

2. Preheat oven to 350°F.

3. Chop almonds into small pieces and brown in 1 tbsp. butter.

4. Mix together the sugar, browned almonds, and cinnamon. Set aside.

5. Generously grease a 6-well muffin pan.

6. On a floured surface, roll each piece of dough into a 4×6-inch rectangle.

7. Using 4 tbsp. of the melted butter, brush just one side of each rectangle of dough with a little butter. Then sprinkle each piece with some of the sugar-almond-cinnamon mixture.*

8. With your fingertips, roll the dough rectangles lengthwise to form logs 6 inches long. Pinch ends together, then form logs into crescent shapes and place in wells of muffin pan.

9. Brush remaining melted butter on each roll.**

10. Cover with a towel (not terry cloth) and let rise for 15 to 20 minutes.

11. Remove towel and bake for 20 minutes, or until lightly browned.

12. Remove from oven and allow to cool in the pan for 5 minutes.

13. Remove each snail from pan and place on cooling rack, glazed side up. Serve while warm.

To reduce the fat content of this dessert, use slightly less butter at this stage. (Please note that the buns will not brown as well.)

**To reduce the fat content of this dish, you can brush the rolls lightly with milk or with lightly beaten egg whites instead of with butter.*

Waiting time (for dough to thaw): 3 hours
Additional waiting time (for dough to rise): 2¾ hours
Preparation time: 40 minutes
Cooking time: 20 minutes
Makes 6 buns

Dinner / Mittagessen

Austrians have traditionally eaten dinner, the biggest meal of the day, at noon. But because many Austrians work outside the home, dinner is often served in the evening during the week. On weekends, however, dinner is usually served at the traditional time. A typical menu would start with a clear broth, followed by an entrée of meat or fish served with dumplings, noodles or potatoes, fresh vegetables, and a salad.

After a heavy meal, Austrians seldom serve rich desserts. Instead, light, fluffy baked delicacies called *Mehlspeisen* are served.

For a tasty, satisfying chicken entrée, try the baked paprika chicken recipe on page 37.

Egg Custard Soup/ *Eierstich Suppe*

This delicious soup is a nice way to begin a festive dinner.

2 eggs

4 tbsp. milk*

¼ tsp. salt

Pinch of nutmeg

1 tbsp. parsley, washed and finely chopped

6 c. water

4 beef bouillon cubes**

1. Preheat oven to 350°F.

2. Combine eggs, milk, salt, nutmeg, and parsley, beating well.

3. Grease two small ovenproof cups or bowls with butter, and pour half of egg mixture into each.

4. Place cups in a shallow pan half filled with water and bake for 25 minutes. Turn off heat, cover cups with foil, and leave in oven for another 15 minutes, until a knife inserted in middle of the custard comes out clean. Remove from oven and cool.

5. Turn out custard and slice into long, thin strips.

6. Bring 6 c. water to a boil, drop in bouillon cubes, and continue to boil.

7. Add custard strips to boiling broth. Turn off heat and cover for 5 minutes.

8. Pour into soup dishes and serve.

*To reduce the fat content of this dish, use skim milk.

**To make this a vegetarian soup, use vegetable bouillon cubes.

Preparation time: 20 minutes
Cooking/baking time: 50 minutes
Serves 4

Paprika Chicken / *Paprika Hendl*

12 pieces skinless chicken, washed
    in cold water and patted dry
    with paper towels

salt and pepper, to taste

paprika, to taste

8 tbsp. butter or margarine, melted

2 c. flour (place in plastic bag)

1 lemon, halved

2 c. hot water

2 chicken bouillon cubes

1 c. sour cream*

*To reduce the fat content of this
dish, substitute some or all of the sour
cream with low-fat yogurt.*

Chicken:

1. Lightly sprinkle chicken with salt, pepper, and paprika.

2. Pour melted butter into shallow bowl. Dip chicken pieces in butter, coating well. Put 2 pieces of chicken at a time in a plastic bag with flour. Close the bag, and shake it gently until chicken is coated with flour.

3. Place chicken in greased baking pan and sprinkle with more paprika, salt, and pepper. Squeeze juice from half a lemon over chicken, then bake at 400°F for 1 hour.

4. Turn oven off. Put chicken pieces on ovenproof serving platter and return to oven to keep warm.

Gravy:

1. Pour drippings from baking pan into a saucepan and heat. Sprinkle 2 tbsp. flour from bag over drippings and stir until brown.

2. Add hot water, bouillon cubes, a pinch of salt, pepper, paprika, sour cream, and juice from other lemon half. Stir until ingredients are blended. Serve with chicken.

Preparation/cooking/baking time: 2 hours
Serves 4 to 6

Breaded Veal/Wiener Schnitzel

Except in Vienna, where boiled beef is popular, Wiener schnitzel is the favorite meat in Austria. The word schnitzel simply means "a sliver," and thrifty cooks make their schnitzels from thin slices of pork or beef. True Wiener schnitzel, however, is a veal scallop.

2 lb. leg of veal, cut into ¼-inch thick slices (ask the butcher to do this)

salt and pepper

½ c. flour

3 eggs, well beaten with 3 tsp. oil*

2 c. fine bread crumbs

¾ c. vegetable oil

Garnish:

2 lemons, each cut into 4 sections

fresh parsley sprigs

baby tomatoes

*You can use an egg substitute to reduce the amount of cholesterol.

1. Pound veal slices with a meat hammer until very thin (about ⅛-inch thick), then sprinkle with salt and pepper.

2. Place flour into a shallow dish and dip veal slices into flour. Shake off excess flour. Dip veal into egg mixture, then roll in bread crumbs, coating well, and set aside.

3. Heat ¼ c. oil in a large skillet, then add as many veal slices as will fit.

4. Cook over medium heat 4 to 5 minutes on each side, or until browned. Remove veal from pan and place on paper towels to remove excess oil.

5. Repeat, adding more oil as necessary, until all veal slices are browned.

6. Serve on a preheated platter garnished with lemon wedges, parsley, and baby tomatoes. After serving, squeeze lemon over schnitzel.

Preparation time: 45 minutes
Cooking time: 30 minutes
Serves 6 to 8

Trout Vienna Style/Bachforellen nach Wiener Art

Although Austria has no seacoast, it has many lakes and streams, so freshwater fish are plentiful. Trout is the favorite. This recipe can be served with cooked potato salad (recipe on page 43).

4 fresh trout fillets, washed, cleaned, and patted dry with paper towels

salt and pepper to taste

1 c. flour

10 tbsp. butter*

6 oz. slivered almonds

2 lemons

1. Lightly sprinkle the trout with salt and pepper.

2. Spread flour on sheet of waxed paper and roll the trout in it, coating well. Shake off excess flour.

3. In a large skillet over medium heat, melt 6 tbsp. butter.

4. Place trout in skillet and cook 5 to 7 minutes on each side, or until golden brown.

5. While trout is cooking, melt remaining butter in a small skillet. Add almonds, stirring until they turn golden brown.

6. Place trout on preheated platter, and pour butter and almond mixture over them.

7. Slice lemons into quarters and serve with each fillet.

Preparation time: 30 minutes
Cooking time: 10 minutes
Serves 4

* To reduce the fat content of this dish, fry the trout in olive oil.

Potato Noodles / *Schupfnudeln*

4 medium baking potatoes, washed and not peeled

I c. flour

I egg

3 tbsp. farina

½ tsp. salt

2 qt. water

4 tbsp. butter (or canola oil for lower fat content)

2 tbsp. parsley, chopped

1. Put potatoes in a saucepan and cover with water. Bring to a boil, reduce heat, and simmer for 20 minutes.

2. Drain potatoes, refrigerate until cold, then peel.

3. Force cold, peeled potatoes through potato ricer or fine sieve into a bowl.

4. Add flour, egg, farina, and salt. Stir together, then knead with well-floured hands into a hard dough, adding more flour if needed.

5. Turn dough onto a floured surface and shape into a log about 2 inches in diameter. Then cut into ¼-inch slices.

6. Using floured hands, roll each piece between fingers, leaving the middle thick and tapering the ends.

7. Bring 2 qt. of water to a boil in a large pot. Add noodles. Simmer for 7 minutes, or until noodles rise to surface. Then use a slotted spoon to put the noodles into a bowl.

8. Melt butter in a frying pan and sauté noodles until well browned and crisp. Garnish with parsley.

Preparation time: 1½ hours
Cooking time: 30 minutes
Serves 4

Cooked Potato Salad / *Gekochter Erdapfelsalat*

3 large potatoes, washed and peeled

3 slices bacon, chopped*

¼ c. white onion, peeled and
   chopped

2 tbsp. flour

2 chicken bouillon cubes dissolved
   in 1¼ c. hot water

½ tsp. salt

¼ tsp. pepper

2 tbsp. sour pickles, chopped

1 tbsp. spicy brown mustard

1 tbsp. apple cider vinegar

pinch of sugar

1 tbsp. parsley, chopped

1. Place potatoes in a large saucepan and cover with water. Bring to a boil, then reduce heat, cover, and cook over medium heat for 15 minutes.

2. Drain potatoes in colander and allow to cool.

3. Wash and dry pan. Sauté bacon and onion until onion is golden brown.

4. Add flour and stir until lightly browned.

5. Add bouillon, a little at a time, stirring constantly with a wire whisk to make a thick sauce.

6. Add remaining ingredients, except parsley and potatoes, and turn heat to low.

7. Cut potatoes into ¼-inch slices and add to sauce.

8. Cover pan and simmer for 20 minutes until potatoes are tender.

9. Sprinkle with parsley and serve.

Preparation time: 30 minutes
Cooking time: 40 minutes
Serves 4 to 6

*For a meatless salad, omit the bacon.
For extra flavor, try substituting
flavored tofu for the bacon.

Broccoli Salad with Bacon/
Brokkolisalat mit Speck

5 stalks broccoli, tender top parts only, washed and cut into small stems

1 small red onion, peeled and sliced into rings

2 slices bacon, chopped and fried*

2 tbsp. apple cider vinegar

½ tsp. salt

¼ tsp. pepper

dash of sugar

2 tbsp. semi-hard white cheese, such as Swiss, grated

1. Using a steaming basket, steam broccoli until barely tender, about 5 minutes. (You can also microwave broccoli with 1 tbsp. water for 4 minutes.)

2. Remove broccoli from basket or microwave, cool, and place in a salad bowl.

3. Add remaining ingredients except cheese, then toss.

4. Sprinkle with cheese prior to serving.

Preparation time: 20 minutes
Cooking time: 10 minutes
Serves 4

*Omit the bacon to make this a vegetarian (and lower fat) dish. To replace the flavor of the bacon, try substituting the bacon with a flavored tofu.

Cucumber Salad / Gurkensalat

2 large cucumbers, peeled and thinly sliced

I tsp. salt

½ white onion, peeled and minced

¼ tsp. white pepper

2 tbsp. apple cider vinegar

I tbsp. vegetable oil

I tbsp. chives, chopped

2 tbsp. sour cream*

1. Place cucumber into a bowl, add salt, mix, then let stand for 20 minutes.

2. Drain liquid from cucumbers, squeezing out excess, and return to bowl.

3. Add remaining ingredients, toss well, and keep cool until ready to serve.

Preparation time: 30 minutes
Serves 4 to 6

Mixed Green Salad / Gemischter grüner Salat

I small head of Bibb lettuce, washed and torn into bite-sized pieces

2 c. fresh spinach, washed and torn into bite-sized pieces

I green onion, washed and chopped

2 slices of bacon, chopped and fried**

¼ tsp. salt

⅛ tsp. pepper

2 tbsp. apple cider vinegar (or lemon juice for a tangier flavor)

dash of sugar

1. Place lettuce and spinach in a large bowl. Add remaining ingredients, toss, and serve.

Preparation time: 20 minutes
Serves 6

*Use plain, nonfat yogurt in place of the sour cream for a lighter salad.

**Omit the bacon to make this a vegetarian dish or substitute smoked turkey meat for the bacon for a low-fat salad.

Cucumber salad is a cool complement to any meal.

Desserts & Pastries/ Mehlspeisen und Gebäck

The Turks attacked Vienna twice in its history, but they never conquered it. However, their beverage—coffee—did successfully conquer the Austrians. *Konditoreien* (shops selling both baked goods and coffee) soon sprang up everywhere, and they are still an important part of social life in Austria. About 3:30 P.M., Austrians stop work to enjoy *Kaffeetafel*, afternoon coffee, and the delicious desserts for which Austria is renowned. After meals Austrians serve light desserts (Mehlspeisen), such as sweet soufflés, rather than rich pastries.

Sacher cake, Austria's famous chocolate cake with chocolate icing, is a dessert few can resist. (See recipe on pages 54 and 55.)

Linzer Cake/Linzer Torte

6 tbsp. melted butter plus 2 tbsp. butter for greasing pan

⅔ c. sugar plus 1 tbsp. for pan

1 egg

1 c. almonds, finely chopped

1 tsp. lemon juice

1 tbsp. milk

2 c. flour

1 tsp. baking powder

1 c. red currant or raspberry jam

1 egg yolk, slightly beaten

¼ c. powdered sugar

1. Mix together the butter, sugar, and egg until creamy.

2. Add almonds, lemon juice, and milk. Sift in flour and baking powder a little at a time, stirring continuously to make a dough, then cool in refrigerator for 1 hour.

3. Preheat oven to 325°F.

4. Generously grease a 9-inch springform pan with 2 tbsp. butter and sprinkle with 1 tbsp. sugar.

5. Divide dough into thirds. Place two-thirds into springform pan. Spread dough evenly on bottom and sides of pan. Spread jam over dough.

6. Divide the last third of dough into 8 pieces. Roll pieces into strips. Place about 1 inch apart across surface of cake in a crisscross pattern.

7. Use a pastry brush to spread beaten egg yolk on top of dough only. Bake for 50 to 60 minutes, until golden brown.

8. Remove from oven, release sides of springform pan, and cool completely. Sprinkle lightly with powdered sugar.

Preparation time: 1 hour
Waiting time (to chill dough): 1 hour
Baking time: 50 minutes to 1 hour
Serves 12

Salzburger Sweet Soufflé / Salzburger Nockerln

This soufflé, the airiest of desserts, is a perfect ending for a festive dinner.

4 eggs, separated*

⅛ tsp. vanilla extract

½ tsp. lemon peel, grated**

2 tbsp. flour

2 tbsp. white sugar

1. Preheat oven to 350°F.

2. In a bowl, stir together egg yolks, vanilla, and grated lemon peel. Then sift flour over mixture and stir gently.

3. In another bowl, beat egg whites with 1 tbsp. sugar until stiff peaks form.

4. Using a rubber spatula, fold egg whites into egg yolk mixture.

5. Generously butter a deep 7×11-inch rectangular or oval baking dish and place four equal parts of the mixture side by side in the dish. Sprinkle lightly with remaining sugar, then bake on middle rack of oven for 12 to 15 minutes, or until the soufflé is lightly browned on the outside but still soft inside. Remove from oven and serve immediately.

Preparation time: 30 minutes
Baking time: 15 minutes
Serves 4

*To separate an egg, crack it cleanly on the edge of a non-plastic bowl. Holding the two halves of the eggshell over the bowl, gently pour the egg yolk back and forth between the two halves, letting the egg white drip into the bowl and being careful not to break the yolk. When most of the egg white has been separated, place the yolk in another bowl.

**Use a cheese grater or lemon zester to remove the yellow peel from the lemon.

Sacher Cake/ *Sacher Torte*

Viennese Prince Klemens von Metternich is partially responsible for the Sachertorte, one of Austria's most famous iced cakes. Created in 1832 by master baker Franz Sacher to please the prince, the cake soon gained popularity. Later, descendants of the master baker built and operated the Sacher Hotel and made this delicious cake their specialty. When a popular Viennese pastry shop copied the recipe, the Sachers took them to court. A historic decision resulted from the famous trial. The Sachers retained their rights under the name Sachertorte, while others would have to call their copies Sacher torte. This delicious iced cake is often served with whipped cream.

Cake:

5⅓ oz. bitttersweet chocolate

1 stick plus 3 tbsp. butter, melted

½ c. sugar

6 eggs, separated

1 c. flour

1 tbsp. baking powder

1 tbsp. powdered sugar

12 oz. apricot jam at room temperature

1. Prepare a 9-inch springform pan by cutting waxed paper the exact size of the base of the pan. (Measure the circle for the base by putting the pan on top of the waxed paper and drawing a circle around it.) Then cut a 29×2¼-inch strip for the sides. Insert waxed paper in pan.

2. Preheat oven to 325°F.

3. In a double boiler, heat the chocolate until melted.

4. In a large bowl, beat butter and sugar. Add melted chocolate, then add egg yolks, one at a time, beating continuously until creamy.

5. In another bowl, sift flour and baking powder together.

6. In a third bowl, using clean beaters, beat egg whites and powdered sugar until stiff peaks form.

7. Add egg whites to chocolate mixture. Sift flour mixture onto egg whites, a little at a time. Fold egg whites and flour carefully into chocolate mixture.

8. Pour into prepared pan, spreading batter evenly. Bake for about 50 minutes. (Test for doneness by inserting a toothpick into cake. If the toothpick comes out clean, the cake is done.)

9. Remove cake from oven, remove springform rim, carefully peel off side paper, and allow cake to cool slightly.

10. Turn onto a cake plate and remove base of pan and waxed paper. Slice cake horizontally, spread bottom layer with jam, and replace top layer.

Chocolate Icing:

7 oz. bittersweet chocolate

1 c. powdered sugar

2 tbsp. butter

a few drops fresh lemon juice

8 to 10 tbsp. hot water

1. Melt chocolate in double boiler.

2. Add powdered sugar, butter, lemon juice, and hot water—one tbsp. at a time—to get right consistency for spreading on a cake. While icing is still hot, spread over top and sides of cake, and allow icing to cool completely.

Preparation time: 2 hours
Baking/cooking time: 1 hour
Serves 12

Supper / Abendessen

When dinner is eaten at noon, the evening meal, or supper, is usually light and simple. It might consist of open-faced sandwiches (*Belegte Brote*) or a variety platter (*Bunte Platte*) of cold cuts, cheeses, and pickled fish. Light meals are served during warmer weather. On cold days, soups and hearty one-pot meals are popular.

Surround colorful tomato baskets with an assortment of salami cones and stuffed eggs to make an attractive supper platter. (See recipes on pages 60 and 61.)

Pork Stew / *Styrisches Schweineres*

This one-pot meal originated in the province of Styria, in the southeast. Since most Styrians work on farms or in vineyards, they like to eat heartily, and this stew satisfies their appetites.

2 tbsp. butter or margarine

1 large onion, peeled and chopped

1 clove garlic, peeled and finely minced

2 stalks celery, washed and chopped

4 large pork ribs, about 2 lb.

dash salt, pepper, and paprika

2½ tbsp. flour

3 c. hot water

1 bay leaf

1 tbsp. apple cider vinegar

2 carrots, washed and cut into pieces

2 potatoes, peeled and cut into pieces

1 small head white cabbage, washed and chopped

¼ c. sour cream mixed with 1 tbsp. milk

1. Heat the butter in a large pot and sauté onion, garlic, and celery until they are golden brown.

2. Put ribs in pot, sprinkle with salt, pepper, and paprika, and brown slightly on each side, pushing onions to side of pot.

3. Sprinkle mixture with flour and stir. Add water, bay leaf, and vinegar.

4. Cover pot, turn heat to low, and simmer for 1 hour.

5. Add carrots, potatoes, and cabbage and continue to simmer for 30 minutes.

6. Remove bay leaf, stir in sour cream/milk mixture and more water if needed. Turn off heat, let mixture set for 5 minutes to blend flavors, then serve.

Preparation time: 45 minutes
Cooking time: 1½ hours
Serves 4

Colorful Variety Platter / *Bunte Platte*

Arrange the tomato baskets in the center of a large wooden or china platter and surround them with the stuffed eggs and salami cones. The Bunte Platte may be garnished with olives, pickles, raw carrots, radishes, cauliflower, asparagus, and tomatoes.

Tomato Baskets / *Paradeiser Körbchen*

4 stalks asparagus, cooked

8 tbsp. whipping cream, whipped

2 tbsp. Parmesan cheese, grated

dash salt and pepper

4 large tomatoes, washed, halved, pulp removed*

paprika, to taste

1. Chop 2 stalks cooked asparagus into small bits and mix in a bowl with whipped cream, cheese, salt, and pepper.

2. Fill tomato halves with equal amounts of asparagus mixture.

3. Cut remaining asparagus in halves, then cut each half into two strips and crisscross them on tomatoes.

4. Sprinkle lightly with paprika.

Salami Cones / *Salami Tütchen*

12 slices hard salami**

4 tbsp. whipping cream, whipped

1 tsp. bottled horseradish

1. Make a cut from the center of each salami slice to the edge, then shape each piece into a cone.

2. Mix whipped cream and horseradish in a bowl, and fill cones with equal amounts of mixture.

*To pulp a tomato, cut the tomato in half and use a paring knife to cut out the pulp.

**Use salami-style tofu to make this vegetarian or use turkey salami for a low-fat option.

Herb-Stuffed Eggs / *Kräuter Eier*

4 eggs, hard-boiled, shelled, and cut in half vertically

2 tbsp. mayonnaise or plain nonfat yogurt

½ tsp. salt

¼ tsp. pepper

I tsp. Parmesan cheese

I tsp. parsley, finely chopped

I tbsp. whipping cream in liquid form

1. Scoop out egg yolks and mash in small bowl.

2. Mix in remaining ingredients, then fill egg white halves with equal amounts of mixture.

Smoked Salmon-Stuffed Eggs / *Lachs Eier*

4 eggs, hard-boiled, shelled, and halved vertically

I½ tbsp. smoked salmon, finely minced

I tbsp. whipping cream, whipped

½ tsp. salt

¼ tsp. pepper

I½ tbsp. sour cream

1. Follow steps for herb-stuffed eggs (above).

Preparation time (entire Bunte Platte): 1¾ hours
Bunte Platte serves 4

Holiday & Festival Food

Gatherings with family and friends to enjoy long, sumptuous meals are an essential part of celebrating holidays and festivals in Austria. Austrian cooks typically prepare meals that are unique to the holiday. Often Austrians prepare dishes commonly eaten throughout the year. By altering them slightly, they turn them into holiday dishes. During Christmastime, for example, Austrians add fruits such as apples to many dishes. They may add apples to salads or to meats such as goose or ham. Austrian cooks often add dried fruits and nuts to breads. To add a lively touch to bread during Easter, Austrians add fruit to dough and braid the bread. During the New Year's holiday, people shape pastries into pig faces to give to family and friends.

The recipes in this section are typical dishes prepared for various Austrian holidays and festivals. Don't let this stop you from making these dishes at any time of the year. Making one of these dishes will surely put you in a celebratory mood. *Guten Appetite!*

Sweeten the season as Austrians do. Chopped nuts, prunes, and dates or figs give this holiday fruit bread (recipe on page 66) its delightful texture.

Bacon Bread / Speckkuchen

In parts of Austria, this bread is served during New Year's festivities. It makes a delicious snack or a light lunch dish served with a green salad.

½ tbsp. sugar

½ c. warm water*

1¼ oz. package active dry yeast

3¾ c. bread flour

¾ c. milk

½ stick unsalted butter

2 large eggs

1 tsp. salt

¾ lb. sliced bacon, diced

*Water should be warm
to the touch.

1. Mix sugar and water, and sprinkle the yeast over the top. Let it rise in a warm place until it bubbles, about 10 minutes.

2. Pour half the flour into a large bowl, making a well in the center.

3. Heat the milk and butter to just before boiling. Pour the yeast and milk mixture into the center of the flour. Gradually beat flour into the mixture to make a thick batter.

4. Lightly beat the eggs with the salt and add to the batter. Gradually pour in the remaining flour. Use just enough flour to prevent the dough from being sticky.

5. Remove to a lightly floured surface and knead for 10 minutes by hand or with an electric kneader until smooth and shiny. Wrap tightly in plastic wrap. Place in a heavy plastic bag, close tightly, and refrigerate.

6. After an hour, unwrap the dough and punch it down with your fist. Rewrap it well and return it to the plastic bag, closing the bag tightly. Leave overnight.

7. The next day, butter and lightly flour two baking sheets. Unwrap the dough, knead it briefly, and divide into two parts. With a rolling pin, roll out one piece of dough into a 12-inch circle.

8. Place on the baking sheet. Evenly press half of the pieces of the diced bacon into the dough. Press each piece well into the dough. Repeat with the other piece of dough. Leave in a warm place, covered with a damp cloth for 20 minutes. In the meantime, preheat oven to 400°F.

9. Bake in the middle of the oven for 20 to 30 minutes, or until golden. Brush the entire surface with the fat that has accumulated around the bacon. Allow bread to cool on a wire rack. The loaf will shrink to approximately 10 inches across.

Preparation time: 1¼ hours
Waiting time: 1 hour and overnight (about 8 hours)
Baking time: 30 minutes
Makes 2 loaves

Holiday Fruit Bread / Kletzenbrot

During holidays in Austria, cookies, cakes, sweet breads, and other pastries are seen and smelled in virtually every home and pastry shop. This fruit bread can be served as part of a festive meal or as a snack.

3 c. flour

⅔ c. brown sugar

3 tsp. baking powder

2 tsp. baking soda

¼ tsp. salt

2 c. buttermilk

1 c. chopped nuts*

1 c. chopped prunes

1 c. diced dates or figs

1 c. raisins

1. Preheat oven to 350°F. Blend flour, brown sugar, baking powder, baking soda, and salt.

2. Add buttermilk slowly, stirring to form a smooth dough.

3. Stir in nuts and fruits.

4. Grease and flour a 10-inch bread pan and spoon batter into the pan. Bake for 45 minutes, remove from oven and let cool.

Preparation time: 30 minutes
Baking time: 45 minutes
Makes 1 loaf

You can use walnuts, almonds, hazelnuts, or another kind of nut.

Fried Carp / Gebackener Karpfen

Fried carp is the traditional main dish at an Austrian Christmas Eve dinner.

3- to 3½-lb. carp fillet

½ tsp. salt

½ c. flour

2 eggs, beaten

½ c. bread crumbs

7 tbsp. canola oil

1 lemon, sliced

1. Wash fish and cut into 4 slices.

2. Sprinkle with salt and let stand for 1 hour in the refrigerator.

3. Put flour, beaten eggs, and bread crumbs into 3 separate shallow bowls or pans.

4. Roll each slice of fish in flour, then eggs, then bread crumbs.

5. Heat oil in frying pan. Fry slices on one side until golden brown (about 5 minutes). Then flip the slices and fry on other side until golden brown (about 5 minutes).

6. Garnish with lemon slices and serve.

Preparation time: 15 minutes
Waiting time (for fish to marinate in salt): 1 hour
Cooking time: 20 minutes
Serves 4

Red Cabbage with Apples / *Rotkraut mit Äpfeln*

Red cabbage is a typical Austrian side dish. During holidays, such as Christmas, people add apples to sweeten this already tasty dish. Red cabbage makes a good accompaniment to a Christmas Day holiday meal of roast goose, potato dumplings, and desserts such as Sacher torte and Christmas cookies.

1 head red cabbage, finely chopped

1 small peeled onion, cut into quarters*

4 to 6 whole cloves

1 large green apple, cut into quarters

2 tbsp. apple cider vinegar

1½ tbsp. sugar

2 tbsp. vegetable oil

1½ tbsp. flour

1. Combine cabbage, onion, cloves, apple, vinegar, ¾ tbsp. sugar, and oil in a large pot.

2. Add enough water to cover the bottom of the pot.

3. Bring to a boil and then simmer until tender, or 1 to 1½ hours. Add boiling water if needed during cooking to maintain enough water at the bottom of the pan to keep the food from sticking.

4. Sprinkle flour and the rest of sugar over the mixture before serving.

Preparation time: 30 minutes
Cooking time: 1½ hours
Serves 6

*For more flavor, cook the onion in oil over medium-low heat before adding the other ingredients.

Index

About the Author

Helga Hughes received her early culinary training at a private college in Forchheim, Bavaria. After moving to the United States, she wrote cooking articles for national newspapers and magazines, and she has written a vegetarian cookbook. This cookbook, however, is about her first love, Austrian cuisine. When not in the kitchen, Hughes follows her other writing interests—exercise and children—and promotes her books.

Photo Acknowledgments
The photographs in this book are reproduced with the permission of: © Robert Fried, pp. 2–3, 15, 24; © Walter and Louiseann Pietrowicz/September 8th Stock, pp. 4 (both), 5 (both), 16, 28, 34, 40, 44, 48, 62, 69; © Robert L. & Diane Wolfe, pp. 6, 39, 47, 51, 52, 56, 59; © Austrian National Tourist Office, p. 11; © Austrian Archives/CORBIS, p. 12.

Cover and spine photos: © Robert L. & Diane Wolfe, front cover (top) and back cover; © Walter and Louiseann Pietrowicz/September 8th Stock, front cover (bottom) and spine.

The illustrations on pages 7, 17, 25, 29, 31, 33, 35, 36, 37, 38, 41, 42, 43, 45, 46, 49, 50, 53, 57, 60, 61, 65, 66, and 68 are by Tim Seeley. The map on page 8 is by Bill Hauser.